Praise for *Payme*

". . . searingly honest . . . punctuated verse with an inborn sense of oral delivery. That Connolly should reprint her poems for the stage seems as instinctive . . ." —Mary Anne Welch, *Mpls.St.Paul*

". . . [a] poetic distillation of the human heart in all its marvelous/mad mystery, its splendor and its sadness. You must read Carol Connolly's crystalline words to let her unique spirit and voice work their magic on you."
—Nadine Strossen

"There is a cathartic air to [Connolly's] verse, which blends humor, wisdom, bravery and a dash or two of melancholy and anger . . . *Payments Due* is a rich, varied terrain."
—Peter Vaughan, *Minneapolis Star Tribune*

"Carol Connolly is a woman of few words—but she makes them count." —Seán T. Kelly, *The Irish American Post*

"Sharp, often wry moments vividly rendered."
—Christopher Meeks, *Daily Variety*

"Strips away lies." —Bruce Feld, *Drama-Logue*

"All the poems are gritty, honest, and make you want to laugh to keep from crying."
—Dave Wood, *Minneapolis Star Tribune*

"There are poems here I very much enjoyed for their humor and strength of form/meaning." —David Ignatow

"About claiming your space . . . potent poems."
—Carla Waldemar, *Minnesota Women's Press*

"Hard-thought poems—not of loose word stones but of rock—surprising observations, images, and metaphors. Don't read if you are afraid." —Eugene J. McCarthy

Payments Due

CAROL CONNOLLY

Carol Connolly

Payments Due

ONSTAGE OFFSTAGE

MIDWEST VILLAGES & VOICES • 1995

Some of these poems first appeared in the *Lake Street
Review* and *Sing Heavenly Muse.*

Midwest Villages & Voices
Post Office Box 40214
Saint Paul, Minnesota 55104

For the women and men
who inspired these poems
and for the artists
whose generosity and talent
gave them life and voice.

Contents

Foreword

When I first read Carol Connolly's poetry, I was delighted to find a writer who wrote the way she spoke. Her keen eye for color and detail, curve and line, space and solid, is always present for anyone who has a conversation with her. Add her wonderful humor, especially in a final line, its twist of reality, a spin of irony making life suddenly bearable, and you have Carol's unique view of the world.

She's looking through the eyes of a woman in her middle years. As a girl, she was good, trusting, obedient, accepting the roles offered her. As a woman, she began to notice other roles, other possibilities. She found the double standard, the discrimination against women, the violence against women, the pervasive discounting of women, and the powerlessness of women. It is a gift to us that she chose to write her poetry and express her rage as well as her love.

Payments Due has been a catalyst for women from every walk of life. It has been passed around in women's groups, read on construction sites, and quoted in courtrooms. In her first edition of this book and in her many readings across the land, Carol's poetry has helped women express their anger and has soothed the pain for women who have felt deserted and betrayed. Carol tells us about her own pain and the pain of many women, and she helps us laugh at ourselves, strengthening us for what's ahead.

The transformation of *Payments Due* into a theatrical presentation has given these poems another dimension for our time of self-discovery and empowerment. The Inner City Cultural Center in Los Angeles has staged a selection of Carol's poems in a multicultural production, and the Lyric Theatre in Minneapolis has mounted its interpretation. The poems performed in these dramatic productions, including a dozen new poems, have been gathered in

"Onstage," the first section of this revised edition of *Payments Due*. Midwest Villages & Voices is grateful to these two theatres for their visionary and supportive work, making visual and audible the written word. And so art and truth and life carry us to deeper understanding and ever more connections.

Rachel Tilsen
Midwest Villages & Voices

Onstage

Performance

The stage setting is a cabaret. A large mirrored ball hangs from the ceiling. At one side is the bar, and on the opposite side is an old round-topped jukebox. The tables are cluttered with empty glasses and beer bottles. It is past closing time, and the place is deserted.

Several women enter: waitresses, a bartender, and the manager. They are all wearing white blouses or sweaters and black skirts or trousers, but their ages are as varied as their racial and ethnic backgrounds. The manager sits at one of the tables and begins making entries in her ledger, the bartender tidies the bar, one woman sweeps the floor, and the others clear the tables. Their tired movements show that their feet are sore and their backs ache, after another night of loud and unruly customers. This is the "magic hour," when co-workers have a chance to relax together before going home.

Presently the women speak the following poems.

Payments Due

Armed with a full list
of infallible rules,
I was finished
in a convent school
where ladies do not speak
of dollars or cents.
I ambled on
to other exclusive shelters,
white linen, white flowers,
and shade.
In the end
it all exploded.
And I was born.
Late.
Yelling and struggling
into the real world
of debits and credits,
bid and ask,
payments due
or else.

You. My hero.
Tall, suave, and smug.
You stepped in
to fill the hole
in my heart.
You flex your muscles
within my womb,
hold your breath
just above water.
Neglect your mortgage
and fold at foreclosure.
Your dry feet do not touch ground.
Smoke from your flame
grows dangerously dense.
My rules said you
would take care of me.

Fantasy Dancing
FOR THE GHOST OF THE IVAR THEATRE

The loneliness was piercing
when you left.
I began to worship idols,
baubles, bangles, whiskey, blow,
searching for you
or someone like you
to love me.

I used what I had,
what was left
of my once perfect body
and I gave it to you
in every way I knew,
coy moves, narrow moves,
writhing, weaving, wide moves.

I sat still for your camera
as you took images of
my small breasts
my long thighs
away with you,
leaving me diminished.
You never said beautiful.

You never said pretty.
You never said, never said.
You only whistle,
shriek,
from behind the footlights.
I can see
two fingers in your mouth.

Your other hand is hidden.
You whistle
an unnerving assaultive
screeching
silence.
I am waiting for you.
Waiting,

waiting. I numb my nerves,
I still my stage fright
with whiskey and blow,
nowhere to go,
pacing, bumping, grinding,
almost believing
that you are watching.

I am waiting for you.
Baubles and bangles,
whiskey and blow.
I stand
afraid
in the cold glare
of the footlights

on the edge of darkness
deep in your shadow,
nowhere to go,
like an animal
looking back,
waiting
for the last blow.

Telling myself this isn't so bad.
Telling myself this is Hollywood.
Telling myself if I do it just right,
if I withstand the silence
for just a little longer,
leave the light
or leave reality,

never stop dancing
never stop
never stop
never,
I am waiting for you
or someone like you
to love me.

Once I sent a bundle of flowers to myself,
a bounteous bouquet of roses
and roses and sweet-smelling roses,
placed them in front of the long mirror,
bragged
that they were from you.
I am trying to believe it's true.

I am waiting for you
or someone like you
to love me.

In the beginning I had dreams.
My star would shine on the big screen,
and if you didn't find me,
some producer, some powerful somebody would.
The bundle of flowers
died during the night. Even
as my hope in their rosy fantasy grew, even

as I did it just right,
bumped with just the right verve,
the sweet-smelling roses died,
curling into themselves, fading,
withering, shriveling,
and I am waiting for you
or someone like you

8

to love me.
There were boys
who smelled of the fields.
There were pitiful old men
who smelled vaguely of disease
and stag, stale urine.
I faced the filth

and the piano man every day
at midmorning. He played
woodenly. I danced
woodenly on the cold floor,
waiting for the next drink,
the next fix,
the next release

waiting for you
or someone like you
to love me.

Waiting for you to come.
For a while the whiskey and blow
made me feel beautiful,
made me believe I was good
in spite of your silence
that growls and rises in the dark
from the gummy scum-stuck

seats in this dank hall,
in spite of the insults you hurl
about my sagging this,
my wrinkling that, my fading,
withering, shriveling.
In the end I swallow
your loathing of me.

I believe you.
I can't wait
any longer
for you to love
for you
or someone like you
to love me.

I take men upstairs,
but I never let them
spend the night.
I don't want
to wake up
with some stranger
in my bed.

I am waiting for you
or someone like you
to love me.

A woman died here
of boredom and neglect.
There is no you.

There is only me.
If it is to be,
it's up to me.

Tightrope

You walk a tightrope alone.
No one can help you.
Anyone who holds your hand
might be out for murder.

If a tall mysterious acrobat,
just the right wave in his dark hair,
comes to you gathering silence
like a marathon runner,
says he can tame lions,
make molehills out of monsters,
curl your hair, cure your nightmares,
says he owns a net,
says his net is new,
you might chance touching his fingers.

If you put your hand in his,
oh! it is warm and strong!
you could lose your balance.
You must walk a tightrope alone.

The Empty Drawer

Its yellow eye stares at you.
An empty drawer left open,
a room stripped,
waiting for the painter.
A porch light burning after midnight.
It stares at you from a dark house.

It hums. A train in the distance,
moving slowly. You watch it,
a train going south without you.
It hums in women's voices
from a television, unwatched
in the next room.
Hums from a telephone
that rings a wrong number.
Hums and whines,
a mosquito on a quiet night.

It sits next to you
in an empty theatre seat.
Its cold hands bind your arms to your sides.
It stalks about a crowded room,
follows you, turns laughing voices
into an icy waterfall.

You say softly and simply in sadness,
"I am lonely."
He says as he smiles, smokes a cigarette,
shuffles the pages of yesterday's news,
swaggers with his baggage,
he says,
"It's bad taste to take anything too seriously."

A Gentleman's Invitation

Meet me at six o'clock
at the New French Café.
We will share,
says he,
a cup of consommé.
Handsome is he
and debonair.
His smile is as wide
as the English Channel.
But a hungry woman
searching for substance
could
drown
in a cup of consommé
at six o'clock
at the New French Café.

What If

A woman with thick ankles knows early
   that she has no power.

What if a pebble hits my windshield
   and continues on
   through my
   left eye, or
what if you write a hit song
   and leave me for a blond
   girl with slender legs,
   tan like bamboo, or
write a hit play
   and leave me for a blond
   boy with slender legs,
   tan like bamboo, or
what if your oil well gushes
   and you
   leave me for
   a cowgirl.

What if you leave and never return,
   and, worse,
   what if you return
   and never leave.
I fear being alone, but
   what if I tell you that
   even more
   I fear never being alone.
You say your vows are true.
   You hold me,
   murmur low,
   promise me stars,
but where will you be tomorrow?
   What if I can't find a place to park?

Even-Numbered Years

This nightmare recurs
more often
in even-numbered years.
You bring words set to music,
white flowers,
dance before me,
tell me you worship
the curve of my hip,
the touch of my cool white hand.
I run in place,
whistle to scramble your sounds,
wipe the sweat from my palms,
stop at last
for air,
and your music takes over.
Slowly I bend to you,
lock my eyes into yours,
and you methodically,
using the principles of logic
and philosophy,
prove to me
I am an asshole.
Prove I indulge myself
in a piercing lack of integrity
and strange beliefs
about the right to happiness.

Watch me now.
I will indulge myself,
love-hate you with a volcanic rage
hotter than your mouth,
prop up what little integrity
I keep buried with the bones of birds,
and warn you. Never come to me again.
Your white flowers have wilted.
They always do.

Welcome

You understand that nothing ends.

A piper plays an Irish tune.
You hear its winter wail for days.
Someone promises
to be your friend for life.
You bury him.
The priest in one breath
without comma without pause
chants and begs mercy
for those who know death
or loss of love.

On a bright green day
you step through a new door.
A lady says in greeting,
"I want to warn you.
Your husband is here.
With another woman."
You blink.
He divorced you.
The judge said it was final
three years ago.

On Park Avenue

1

At breakfast
on Park Avenue
darling Deirdre
said to the countess,
smiling graciously,
words slipping like jewels
through her straightened teeth,
"Mother, Stepfather and I
have an announcement.
We are going to be married."
Mother's grief and rage seeped
through the many floors
of the apartment
on Park Avenue,
drizzled like hot rain
on the Puerto Rican janitor
as he wrung the necks of
white chickens
raised among the topiary trees
and blooming rare red roses.
White chickens
squawking, squawking,
on Park Avenue.

2

My good man,
on your island
it may be
de rigueur to keep
livestock
in one's quarters.
It simply
is not done
on Park Avenue
at any time.
Luncheon
on Park Avenue
was conducted
behind windows
banged shut
closed tight
against the
squawking
squawking
to keep
some semblance
of order
on Park Avenue.

3

At dinner
on Park Avenue
the countess invited friends
and the newly coupled
to celebrate,
a show of her acceptance
of the breakfast announcement
to be played out
at dinner
on Park Avenue.
Aroma of lovely things simmering slowly,
candle flames dancing
on crystal holding blood red wine,
heirloom china gleaming
on the snow white table,
ready for the celebration
at dinner
on Park Avenue.
The centerpiece was the countess mother
gracefully draped in pale silk, arms crossed
and throat slit
straight, so straight,
silver knife in her right hand,

her burgundy blood
staining
the perfect white carpet
at dinner
on Park Avenue.

Surrender to Henri Bendel

In white rooms
filled with the white notes
of heavy metal,
everyone wears white
with their tan.
A tiny dark woman,
her face intricately scarred,
takes my hand and leads me
to water.
This is a beauty shop.
She speaks only Iranian, *darling,*
her assistant speaks only Chinese, *darling,*
and their idea of beauty
and mine
may not be the same.
There is no way of knowing.

Mirror, Mirror

The morning news is brought to you by
the national association of stutterers.
Umbrellas bloom like violets
on Fifty-seventh Street.
At the coffee shop forty-two chickens turn
on seven spits, sputter in the heat.
He announces that I must improve. Firm
up. Consider a face lift. He tells me he
has seen women become man's best
friend after a lift. Okay,
I consider it. I learn to spell
Ponce de León, and for a while
I never pass a mirror without stopping
to push at my forehead, my eyes,
pull at my throat, stare
at the possibilities of youth,
confront myself from every sagging side,
and in the end, I know. The best
way to improve is to
stand alone. Take time
to practice my pirouette as I
turn to embrace age
with the same gusto
I squandered youth.

Last Resort

I am trapped here in a second-rate body.
I. Me with the proper address
and acceptable blood lines
and the appearance of a decent bank balance.
Trapped here at the pool
during the thigh show.
Sins of the flesh
are punished here. Exposed.
Sagging tits and a stretched belly
negate a person at this spa.
Here the only interest is in bones
and sinew and teeth and tan.
No flesh need apply.

Attention. Over here. I would
like to say that I am terribly sorry
if I have visually assaulted you.
I want to explain. I followed the rules.
It was seven pregnancies for me
and twins and nine-pound babies,
and do you know?

If you want to have your cake,
you must eat it.

An Ordinary Event

The fact that it happens
to all of us
doesn't make it any easier.

I turned a corner,
and suddenly
without warning
I stand full
before a mirror,
and there it is.
My mother's face
staring back at me
in disbelief.
The face
I swore
I'd never have.

In a Word

A woman I met
briefly,
and only
by chance,
said,
"I like your
boyfriend,
but you are
smarter
than he is."
It had never
occurred to me.
I thought
it over.
He is taller,
stronger,
prettier,
younger,
and she's right.
I am
smarter.
This news
changes
everything.

Shallows

FOR THE 577 DEMONSTRATORS
ARRESTED AT HONEYWELL
ON OCTOBER 23, 1984

I want to float in the shallow water
close to the shore
where the sea is still,
the sand is white.

I want to loll
on my back on a puffed-up life raft,
search for the silver lining,
gaze at the sky as blue as blue,

glide straight into the sun,
and be consoled.
Never look back.
I have been in deep water.

I could
tell you stories
you would not
believe.

I will be alone now,
solitary, celibate.
I don't want to hear even a whisper
of the syllables in *nuclear*,

the hiss in *holocaust*,
the murder in *mutilation*.
I don't want to smell the sweat
in *demonstrate* or *lobby* or *elect*.

The kingfishers will roar by
in speedboats.
I won't even wave.
Far in the distance

the heat shimmers.
You may decide
to board a big boat,
chain your body to a war machine.

Remove all sharp objects
from your pockets
so you won't hurt yourself
or wound the cop who arrests you.

The steel door will bang behind you.
The jailor will say your time begins.
Keep in mind,
what is legal is not,

and as you pour strength
into the deep ocean
that floats my raft close to the shore,
I will be safe in the sun

because you
hold back the dark
with your bare hands.

Gratitude

When the light is right,
the sweet perfume of hyacinths
rolls around me.

I say thanks to everyone
but myself.

I bow low to my mother
buried in 1959,
to my father

buried on the same day,
to my brother
who moved to Edina,

to a husband
who had the sense
to divorce me,

to my children
who followed nature
and grew up,

to the man in a hat
who says he adores me,
to the men who say nothing.

When the sky is dark at noon
and the hyacinths
are dead and dank,

I blame no one
but myself.

Song

FOR RICK AND SONIA

In that lovely tempestuous time, just
at the beginning, even before the first touch,
when you recognize your destiny,
see its beauty, the endless possibilities,
you are extraordinarily happy.
The music was written just for you.

It is a time when lilacs are in bloom
and in the everydays to follow you will
remember this spring. The blossoms are
as profuse as they have ever been.
You are wrapped in a positive conscious choice
like a bird in flight when the air is warm

at sunrise. The sky shimmers. You dance
hand in hand through the square. You sing
your unbridled joy to passersby. You bow
to the persistence of memory. You see
its beauty. You know with certainty
you don't want to be anywhere else.

Song
FOR CYNDY AND ANDY

Sometime after the beginning
on a high balcony, crystal sparkles
in the afternoon sun. In a room
adjacent, someone plays a Gershwin
rhapsody. The piano is in perfect
tune. You embrace with new
intensity, ponder all the times past.

It's true. You danced almost every
dance. Everything slows to a long
curve. You feel alive
and disconcerted. In your heart
you have always known this is the melody
you're after. There is someone
to watch over you. It is

time to sing your song.

It was the driest May in history.
June brings soft rains in early morning.
The gardens flourish. You find
your sensitive soul has a need
to gather larkspur and white tulips
in great bunches. Luck stands
firmly at your side. It is

time to sing your song.

Time to uncover your true design.
Time to croon to the long hot days
of this perfect summer, traipse
through fields of promises forever.
Larkspur, white tulips, and perfect
pink roses forever. It is

time to sing your own song.

29

Family Values

To further an ambition,
his, not mine,
and to even the score

one last time,
I have moved
into seven hundred and fifty square feet,

an inch of grease on the stove,
cracked cups shattered plates stuffed
behind the refrigerator, the sink

is alive with cockroaches,
and on Saturday last
when I turned on the gas,

water gushed. It shot all over.
I scrubbed on my hands and knees
for several days, rearranged

three boxes of Rawlings baseballs
one closet seven cupboards eleven drawers
a gross of mismatched socks.

I never stop watching him.
He grows ever more peculiar.
Even the atmosphere is fertile,

and, of course, the use of force
is always a possibility.
Crashing thrashing all that blood,

a brand-new baby boy.
I am not stupid. I vow
to become a vegetarian.

I have moved
into enough places
to know.

The blind woman
sitting on the bus bench
rocks to and fro.

And Then It's Who You Know

FOR BRIGID ON HER EIGHTEENTH BIRTHDAY

The moon dances tonight,
swings her veils in a wide circle.
Her smile is bold, full of promise,
for she knows

the first and most perfect
of figures is the circle.
Even as you embrace this
incontrovertible wisdom,

contemplate the effect
of gravitational forces.
Begin to cultivate
a defiant attitude.

Question everyone. There is
a vanishing point. Ask,
would your method work
if the circle passed through

its origin? Would it be
consistent with everything else
you know? Will it remain
constant over the years?

Perhaps you will become
a pacifist to passionate
inquiry, but even if you
slip into this category,

continue to cultivate
a defiant attitude, and keep
in mind that in spite of forces
beyond your control

the circle is infinite.

Blue Covers

My third son,
the charming one,
the toker,
dope smoker,
keeps his reefer papers
with his lunch tickets
between the blue covers
of his algebra text,
blue as his eyes,
as blue as the Irish river
that runs through my soul.
No grades in algebra for him.
His brains are going up in smoke.

I have wrung my hands
through car wrecks,
stolen checks,
failing grades,
and promises made,
then broken.
He comes to
just long enough
to blubber
that he has lost my trust.

Yes.
And he is about
to lose my interest.

Man's Best Friend

In the center
of the Empire
men dress in fine ensembles
and walk the dog.
They bend beneath curbs,
gather warm dog excrement
in clear bags pulled
from fine silk pockets.
Only the finest.
This is the center
of the Empire,
where money
talks
and dogs are walked
on Gucci leashes
and dog dirt
is collected.
E is for Empire.
Its excellence
is elegant,
but excrement
exists.
In piles.

The Index

If you shake your finger at me again,
I will bite it off and hold the tip
in my teeth until I die.
People with
police power
will find it.
Trace you.
You will be
arrested.
In Duluth.

On the Study of Mythology

When, at last, she took
a good look at Medusa,
she began to understand.

A man can be
in terror of a woman.
Buried in his marrow

is the ancient fear
of falling slowly
into her dark recesses,

tumbling
rolling
disappearing

part by part,
hat first,
until all that remains

is one wing-tip oxford,
shoelace dangling
on the white sheet.

It's Not Going Well

Five years
of one man's adoration
and undying devotion
is enough for anyone.
When I told him I
wanted to separate,
he leapt like someone
shot.
Now the whole house
smells of wounded buffalo,
and he continues
to serve tea
in the best china
exactly
at midnight.

Is This a Joke

He invited a student to live in their house,
to work in exchange for lodging.
He began to take brandy to bed,
to cover the glass with a paperback book
to save it from evaporation during the night.
His wife woke him,
shook his shoulder. She asked,
"Do you love the student more than me?"
He resisted, feigned sleep,
rustled the sheets, groaned,
and finally resigned himself
to a true/false answer.
"Yes."
His wife announced
she would now kill herself,
put her head in their oven.
As she turned from their marriage bed,
her elbow tipped the brandy.
It bled into the pages of his soft book.

After some blank time,
with nothing to read or drink,
he ventured to their kitchen.
Curious, he wondered if she knew:
to suicide
you must blow out the pilot light.
"How is it going?"
His wife, her golden hair dull
with carbon and sweat, said,
"It's hot in here."

Romance

In every romance
there is a time, early,
when I want to consume him,
own him,
lock him in a closet in my vicinity.
A closet with a window.
I am not a killer.
I want to put him in a box,
carry him with me,
and if he, without looking,
steps into the box,
I close the cover quickly,
bang it shut,
and hang it with a heavy padlock.

As I turn the key in the lock,
I look at him curled in the box
and think,
"You idiot. What are you doing in that box?"

Mailman

I waited each day, through
an hour locked in yellow light,
stood at attention,
and watched for the clock to read 10:00.
Around ten the mailman rings the bell.
I hoped with excruciating intensity,
fingers tightly crossed,
for some word from you,
some small curl from your pen.
Now you are with me.

This morning I watch you.
You annoy me.
You came here to ruin ten o'clock.
You make the mail nothing.

Goodbye
FOR DOROTHY PARKER

I wouldn't like to be
the Queen of Romania,
rule the land or stand
in ceremony, serene
in the face of confusion,
but I would, yes,
I would like to see
the Queen of Romania
sitting straight
in the first box
at the new World Theatre,
her hat scrolled in gold,
ornate as the pillars
supporting her pedestal.
I would stare at her,
savor every detail.
I would, yes,

I would like to leave
you slumped
in the balcony
and sit close
to the Queen of Romania,
face forward, hear
the music, clutch
my pocketbook and walk
with the Queen of Romania
to the exit.
I would, yes,
I would wave
graciously
as you
disappear
through a hole
in the night.

Diary

He shakes his finger
and wails
that I have
written long passages
in his private diary.
I say I'm sorry.
I didn't think.
And don't you worry.
I wrote in pencil.
I don't admit
that I pressed
as hard as I could
on his fine white paper
near the back
where the pages were blank,
close to the blood red cover.
No amount of erasing
will take me
out of his book.

The Affair

When we met, we knew.
When we met anew,
we knew we knew.
Then I brought my children,
and you were drunk.
Dead ends do end in
dead ends.

Balancing Act in Midlife

The moon is high. Your bronze
satin would shimmer
in this abnormal heat,
sweat rosebuds as you move
your hands, your mouth.

You vow this
intense new
moonlight
blinded you
at first sight.

I watch the leaves on my tree
turn purple slowly. It is
October, time for harvest,
and you are in the bayou.
My hat is tethered here.

We do the great moonbeam
balancing act,
juggle the brilliance
between us. My hand
is steady when you call.

You say the leaves
on all the trees
in your town
have been purple
for some time now.

Wind-Chilled Town

You come to me from the steamy mist
of a torrid zone,
but you are
gone
before you arrive. Still,

I hear your voice when
I comb my hair, the faint roll
of your *r.* You say
there is something strange
between us. You say

there is a fleck of deep
purple in my eye. You say
you don't give a damn
about New Orleans. You say
you only want to be

in my wind-chilled town.
I wait in black and white
intensity.
My hand is on my heart.
I wait to hear you sing

tunes of totems,
tell tales of triumphs.
I wait to savor every
succulent syllable. You
swagger in. Your hat

is flat. Your song is boiled
to a stale, familiar mush.
I wait now, I wait, I wait
for you to leave.
I want to comb my hair.

Divorced

I am alone,
single,
solitary,
separated,
celibate.
I have borne eight children.
I worry now that I will die
a virgin.

Celebration

I hear news
of a thirty-seventh
wedding anniversary
and think,
My god.
It would be nice.
In case either party
requires any sort of amputation,
there will be
no need
for anesthetic.

Ntozake Shange Visits Minnesota

Life is limitations.

Woman, brilliant, exotic woman,
reads her poems full of color and wild movement,
says she began to read in saloons
when she was nineteen.

At nineteen I was looking for a career to marry,
reading Amy Vanderbilt and Emily Post.
I knew nothing of poetry.
I blame the nuns.
They never mentioned poems.

All the best poets are divorced.
Exotic woman embraces her culture,
sees its flaws
and celebrates.
If her elders told her to cross her legs
and bind her breasts,
she paid no attention.
She smokes Kools in a chain,
chants of love and rape,
of freedom, commandos in brown boots,

abstracts time in countries I can't spell.
I watch this woman stomp out
golden words and silver.
I know that life is limitations,
and I don't like it.
I slip into wishing I had a Milky Way to bite,
its wrapper stamped "Satisfaction Guaranteed,"
fill my mouth with its sweet soft brown mass, fill it,
and leave no room in my head
for the knowledge that

life is limitations.

Lady Poet at Lunch

At a small table of big-time poets,
leaning into their strong winds,
she politely waves the clean vowels,
the polished consonants of her smallest poems.
Unheard.
Contemplates a table knife through a heart,
a fork plunged into an open hand,
knows the Irishman would see
the beginnings of stigmata,
wishes instead for paper pom-poms
to act the proper
cheerleader.
Pom-poms
to whish rah-rah,
as expected, and yet maintain
the required silence.
Rah-rah.
Silent sis-boom-bah.

Afterwards, safe in her kitchen,
she waits
for her new skin to thicken,
says time spent with the big time
may be time misspent,
feels invisible,
and her son says, "Invisible?
But you look nice."

Without a Hat

If you are
not a blessed virgin
but an ordinary woman
full of ordinary dreams
on an ordinary night,
full of wine and expectation
when the moon is high,
you might find a handsome athlete
and dance slow with him,
sway a little to his song,
and go with him
for just a little while.
But should he gather others,
make an all-American trio
who lock you with their
music in a plain room,
taunt you
and ridicule you
as they abuse you,
take their turns
all night, all night,
at hurting you so bad,
so bad,
all that will remain in you is
one scream
and you will cry

for help.
Help.

Then you will be required
in extraordinary ways,
again and yet again,
to explain
why you
are just an ordinary woman
and not a blessed virgin.

Fantasy

If my breasts were
as sharp and pointed
as the pyramids,
I would use them
to cut
red *x*'s
in his face.

Lizzie Borden

"Lizzie Borden took an ax
And gave her mother forty whacks.
When she saw what she had done,
She gave her father forty-one."

I understand you, Lizzie Borden.
You end it, forty whacks
with a cleaver or an ax,
say no to the vows,
give the contract a decent burial,
plant white flowers,
move on,
check your bags
with any handy porter,
and still
a long first marriage stays with you,
a mark on your soul
like mother's words
and father's warnings,
wanting extreme unction.

You see the reflection of your own face
in a cloudy mirror that won't come clean.

My Sisters

ON THE TENTH ANNIVERSARY
OF THE DFL FEMINIST CAUCUS

When madness descends,
wraps itself around my legs,
begins to paralyze me,
you, my sisters, hold me
on this side of the fine line
that divides sunlight
from insanity.
You are the warmth of spring
to my frozen field,
the summer rain
to my drought.
You are the moon
in my midnight.
Your steadfast wisdom
surrounds me
in circles that ripple out
and hold my daughters
and their daughters
in a place where
the sun shines brightest
and strength
blooms,
awesome in its beauty.

You Were Something More Than Young and Sweet and Fair

FOR LEE NORMAN

She is my mother,
my daughter,
my sister.
She is a new woman,
an old woman,
a wise woman.
She is a legator of
faith and hope and generosity.
She puts her hand to strong things,
and she is clothed with strength and dignity.
She laughed at the days to come.
She is all of us,
and part of her is none of us,
for she is one in her talent
and her wisdom and her gift for giving.
We call her friend,
and the sun, with its face shining,
remembers her.

Ostrich Egg

She kept her life in an eggshell,
tended it carefully.
A pale blue shell,
ornate with gold leaf.
Safe, she thought,
in her airtight oval.

On a June night
he thrust out a leg.
Deep in sleep,
he flung his leg across her,
cracked her shell beyond repair.
Some said righteously,
he was violent.

She began to sleep alone,
emerging slowly
as the rupture
in her tended shell
grew wider.

She was last seen
smiling in a broad new way,
her lungs expanding
like sails full of strong winds.

Offstage

Sixth Street

The clouds are blown off.
We sit here on the dark side of the house.
The truth stands silent between us,
at attention,
heels of its worn shoes pressed together.

In fighting everydayness
I sought a Sunday sort of man.
Oh, how the sun shone from him.
Today the rain persists.
Through the transom I see

five chimneys atop five row houses
that rise through the wet lilacs.
The clock shows 5:05.
People who pull the petals from daisies
should part at an uneven hour.

The door that swings both ways
opens and closes tight.
You say goodbye at 6:06.
I have been in this cave before,
fingered every inch.

I know it is the same garden
before and after the storm,
and a wildflower that appears to be
finished
renews itself without invitation.

A Small Plug for Big Cooling

Not humidity. Heat.
Some vegetable gardens are in trouble.
Soft rotted bottoms.
Male flowers drop off.
There are not enough bees around,
and vine borers spread the disease.
Make notes.
Consider an insecticide.

A return of normal
growing weather
should set things right.

On the Confines of Marriage

"Save 20% on our collection of
Legant Diamonds!"
the advertisers command
in typographical error.
They will have to find an *e*.
Will they take it from
he or from *she*?
The *e*.
Whose pronoun will it deplete?

Tarnish

Her flesh hot from a morning
on the desert,
she steps over the stone hedge
of sharp words and silence
piled between them
in the days just past.
He opens his arms to her.
She clings to him,
whispers of her want,
begs for the comfort
of his body,
and he says,
"As soon as I have my toast."

He wonders aloud as he chews,
tiny dry crumbs trembling on his lower lip,
he wonders
why spoons tarnish
and jam furs.

Turkey

He is a man
more ordinary
than he thinks.
As a child
he ate Wheaties
at Thanksgiving.
Everyone else ate
turkey.
He thought
he might not like
turkey.

Regrets

Wanting you,
not wanting you,
in dread of you,
I tell myself once more
that dozens of daisies
and boxcars of berries
and moonsongs
and marathon dancing
and love given blind with passion
do not make regrets.

Regrets are made of nothing.
Blank spaces and empty places
are mummy cases for a beating heart.
Things undone are bricks
layered on things unsaid,
the dare not taken,
the hand not held,
the gaze not met,
eyes kept dry,
all mortared with quiet
and finished
with code words
prescribed by Emily Post.

Two Babies

I had two babies,
if you count twins as two.
I asked for a warm robe,
something sturdy
to wrap out the chill of 2:00 A.M.
He gave me yards of pink marabou.
He wanted me to be a naive girl
whose dancing would make
the fragile feathers float
up and down.
I wanted the insult
of his foolish feathers
plucked flat
so that no baby would be tickled
except by me.
I wanted him to understand.
Baby care is serious work.

He was a fool,
and so was I.

Long Shadows

My children walk back and forth under the moon.
Their long shadows crisscross in quick *x*'s
and loom before them.
They carry oranges through the snow
and brown sacks of milk and eggs
with no thought to the space not filled,
the long dark empty space before them.

My children. Prepare yourselves.
Say "Thank you" and wipe your feet.
That sweater is too warm.
Don't spill the milk.
Careful with the eggs.
Lower your voices
and watch out for the long shadows.

August

It is a shipboard romance
on land as dry as brown pastures,
a fifteen-day sail through
intemperate zones,
blue rooms, sweet songs,
your green eyes agate hard
with pain not yet abandoned,
and a single tear is trapped
in the stem of your crystal glass
as the catatonia of hard desire
plays out on silent saxophones.

The horizon is bright with a new sun.
We make shadows on a tin bird
and swing on dark porches.
I know there is music in nightlife,
Stoddard will lecture
in brave words, not foolish,
Mars remains,
the world will never end,
and I wonder
if you make outgoing calls
from your sensible black telephone.

Below Zero

Dangerous weather.
Windchill
sixty-five degrees
below zero.
I tell you I have seen, just now,
on the freeway leading from Minneapolis,
thirteen cars stalled,
five cars in one wreck,
and a sports car descending,
taillights in a spiral,
over the edge of a bridge.

You say, "My god,"
the whine of ridicule in your voice,
"life and death within a mile,
a veritable working girl's Vietnam,"
as though the only
valid experience,
this weather, is yours.

Do I still love you?
It's like riding a bicycle.
If I begin again,
I'll be able to do it.

Icebox

His silence separates us,
a sheet of blue ice.
It reflects the light
of my devotion,
dim as a fifteen-watt bulb.
He floods the ice
and sweeps it with secrets
locked like lasers in his eyes.

The oxygen level is low
in this icebox.
No heavy breathing allowed.
No rage. No fury.
No hammering of aching hearts.
No splashing of hot tears.

Keep it still.
If the ice cracks
and begins to melt,
we will rot like chickens
freezer-burned since Christmas.

Late Date at Le Zinc

On the third day
of the third month,
after a week of greetings

and partings
in places polluted
by dangerous decibels,

we meet to part.
The same old shrimp,
antennae paralyzed,

stare once more
from your white plate.
Metal music bounces

off the zinc bar,
hits the tin ceiling,
and shows no mercy.

I want you to understand,
I shout.
I don't blame you,

I shout.
I forgive myself,
I shout,

as you drown
in the pounding waves
of a silly stranger

at the next table.
Her every syllable
is audible.

She describes her
manicure to her
companion. His

hat is in his
hand. I flounder.
You pale, nail by nail.

Dear John

I don't want to think about this,
but sometimes
a memory seeps like steam through
the frozen glass of my pond.

I stood once at the ancient sink
that hangs steadfast on my kitchen wall,
its innards exposed,
held the hand of Brigid,

our seventh born,
stared at the rope of garlic
hung to ward off vampires,
and you said I was a parasite.

Parasite, you said.
Who knows when anything ends.

I see you everywhere these days,
in crowds and couples.
Never is it you. Not once.
I dream you wear a beard.

Brigid says it's true. You do.
And your new sink grinds garbage.
This pale new woman, quiet.
She smokes so many cigarettes.

You call her "fiancée."
Is she a virgin?
I want to know.

Dollars and Cents

Money is the color of mold.
Use it for a poultice
and it will infect your wound.
And you,
you are

bad if you have it,
bad if you don't,
bad if you try to get it,
bad if you refuse it,
bad if you lend it,
bad if you borrow it,
bad if you win it,
bad if you lose it,
foolish if you inherit it,
suspect if you ignore it.

Its fungus creeps
into the corners of marriages,
suffocates sons and daughters.
If you marry for money,
you will earn it.

It Was a Very Mad Affair

There was music between us,
the joy of
clean sweet jazz.
Then you began to beat
your drum in solo.
Hard and fast
you beat it
to a vicious decibel.
The veins in your neck
stood out
blue, like twilight.
I had to cover my ears
and then my eyes.
At last
even you admit it.
You can't take the noise.

I sink slowly,
best foot first,
into serene solitude.
And still
some days I wonder.
Can I take the silence?

Calculator

I know
my numbers
are all wrong.
They divide into
too many years,
an uneven number
of children,
months in cities
where only
local time is observed
and white flowers wilt,
weeks of existing conditions,
absurdities, imprecisions,
days and days and days
misspent,
and you.
You brought me
a string of pearls.
Pearls are nice,
but a woman
with high numbers
should have
a string of zeros,
six or seven
shiny ciphers
hanging
from a simple digit
for comfort
in the dark days
of November,
when the nights
are long.

No Vacancy

Riding all night
past neon signs that blink
"No vacancy."
Closed. No eggs for travelers.
Meeting dawn in a mountain town.
In small houses
close to the road
daily rituals are observed.
Coffee is cooking,
women crack eggs,
men shave in silence,
children stretch and yawn
on the edge of rumpled beds.
I am on the road.
Before the sun brings noon,
I'll stretch my legs
in New York City.
Tomorrow is as fragile
as a sheer curtain pulled tight.
Any old dog
who comes along
can put his paw
through it.

Baggage

There are some things you have to expect.
If you ride on airplanes,
sooner or later
you stand by that great roulette wheel
that spits out baggage
and your number will not come up.
You look back in fondness at past luck,
when misgivings were temporary,
and accept the empty chute.
You don't have a grip.

You are stranded
in New York without a nuance
to call your own.
There may be abuses.
Your well-kept secrets
have escaped into space,
and your permanent point of view
is loose with your toothbrush,
wrapping itself in your reputation.

Reality is something you rise above,
but the longing
to drag your baggage
lingers.

Old Questions

There is a piano here in this new place,
this place that promised new answers to
old questions.
A slim ebony upright piano in the foyer
stands in the shadows gathering city dust.
Steadfast in its stillness, it waits,
calling out in long dark silent *oh*s
for a piano player.
There are few words
from you, here in this new place.

If you were here in this new place,
your sharp and flat notes would
fall all over the rooms here,
wrinkle the smooth sheets,
cover the floors with confetti,
blow out the windows,
bend the trees in Riverside Park,
and splash into the Hudson River.

The coast guard would knock hard at this door,
people in this building would ring me with
complaints,
and the bone-thin woman who holds a mute dog,
her eyes dart about the elevator in search of order,
would have me evicted here
from this new place.

Side Trip from Southampton

The sun blazes,
and there is no shelter
on Shelter Island,
where the deepest blue
hydrangeas, wild in their profusion,
are full blown
just this side of rot.

In the harbor
the air is still.
Sails down, boats
are stacked
like cordwood
in this unrelenting heat.

He promises
to light my cigarettes
with dollar bills.
I don't smoke.
And the marigolds.
A piercing, blinding yellow,
more yellow
and bigger
than I ever remember.

Friday Night Flight

The desert sky at dusk
is painted with a broad brush.
We bend beneath an arch of oleander,
emerge into the confetti
of new stars. Turning
from bells of laughter,
we climb on the Friday night flight
for Purgatory, Arizona.
This began in innocence,

a planned assault on continuity,
a stop in Jerome, where fragile
houses grip the mountainside
on slender stilts. Geronimo
was a teamster here, and then
he was immortalized.
Safeway declares in weathered perpetuity
its pledge to distribution
without waste.

I did not surrender
to his pink shirt.
I was not swayed by his eyes
blue as the desert sky,
by the majesty of red rocks
in the sun of Sedona,
by mountain air sweet
in a field of yellow flowers.
It happened during the night.

He took my hands in his firm grip
and kissed my fingers
in his sleep.

Carefree, Arizona

In a garden pruned, meticulous,
patrolled each day at dawn,
grass kept green in desert heat,
an unfeathered bird intrudes,
prostrate and still
on my threshold
in the sun of Sunday noon.
Translucent skin spreads from its
tiny baby body, wings
outstretched in silent salute
to a parade
of insects moving in
to stand at attention.
Born at sunrise,
dead before noon,
its courage will
never
stand the test
of the chill
that comes in the dark
just before dawn.

No Lolling

No lolling around.
No lolling around in bed.
No lolling on sofas. Or overstuffed chairs.
It was my mother's foremost rule.
I was an energetic loller,
an expert at lolling in and on.
When lounging pajamas came into fashion,
I recognized their acceptable chic.
I never was successful at lounging.
Even now I remain
devoted to sprawled lolling.
Keep in practice.
But I will admit,
since my mother is gone,
I loll
with less verve.

They Say It's a Cliché

One day at dawn you open a window
    on a new city and see
that not much is right
    and in your neighborhood
not much is wrong,
    that some rights are not granted
and some wrongs cannot be righted,
    that money is king
and beauty is queen
    and romance rescues only the naive.
You wrap your arms around the truth
    that you are
        a middle-aged,
        middle-class,
        middle-weight contender
        for a midlife crisis.

Rejection

No thanks for your work,
the editor says.
This requires
two typewritten pages.
Cut your poems up,
he says.
Line by line.
Put the lines together in a hat.
Pull them out.
One at a time.
And see what happens.

Ah. But
I don't
have a hat.

Dilettante

I am a full-time fraud,
passing as a poet.
It's filthy work. But
someone has to do it.
Stilted syllables
line my walls,
confusion
crowds my room
with maggoty mounds
of mediocre metaphors,
ridicule lurks
in my hallway,
ambitious people
take all the best lines,
and I have a headache.
I woke up with it. But
everyone wakes up
with something.

Ode to a Message

She answered the telephone,
said, "Yes, yes,"
and drew a Grecian urn
on the message pad,
the rim of its perfect neck
flush with the paper's edge,
as though to say, "No
to any wildflowers in my urn.
No to any spilling of my wine."

Into the telephone
she hummed, "Of course, yes, yes,"
as she drew a second urn
and then a third,
all in the same position.

The Key

Some of you are winners.
Some of you are losers.
You know who you are.
If you become trapped
in this elevator,
do not
become excited.
Use the phone.
Call security.
The guard will
put a key in his ear,
and wax will lubricate
the mechanism.
A lot of people
are having trouble
with their ears
these days.

Immaculate Corridor

In the locked ward,
from behind a door shut tight,
halting Chopin falls carefully
to the floor,
one perfect chord
ahead of chaos.
Notice: "Music Room
Locked
Midnight to 8:00 A.M."
Scant strength at sunrise
for a sleepless player
without a note
to call his own.
A burn like that
affects your whole system.

Fast Shadows

She is seated in ceremony,
taps her fingers on the table,
casting fast shadows
on the café's linen cloth,
every fiber stretched white.
She slowly crosses her legs.
Never will they know again
the weight of her husband's body.
He abandoned her without notice.
Gave in to a failing heart
on a tennis court in Mexico.
They were there to outwit
the white of winter.
Now once more
she uncrosses her long white widow's legs
and feels the weight
of the quiet loneliness of solitude,
waits for the arrival
of a new man she knows but little.
Stares.
Contemplates cockroaches
and dreads their fast shadows,
the way they appear and disappear
in silence
without notice.

About the Author

Carol Connolly was born, raised, and educated in the Irish Catholic section of Saint Paul, Minnesota, and has seven children. She began writing poetry at the age of forty. She has worked as a columnist for the *Saint Paul Pioneer Press, Mpls. St. Paul* magazine, and *Minnesota's Journal of Law and Politics.* She has been a commentator for KARE Television, an NBC affiliate, and performed in *What's So Funny about Being Female?* at the Dudley Riggs theatre in Minneapolis. She has served as cochair of the Minnesota Women's Political Caucus, chair of the Saint Paul Human Rights Commission, and chair of the affirmative-action committee of the Minnesota Racing Commission. In 1992 Revalyn T. Golde adapted and directed a stage production of *Payments Due* at the Ivar Theatre in Los Angeles. In 1993 and 1994 Larry Roupe directed productions for the Lyric Theatre in Minneapolis. Roupe has said of *Payments Due,* "I fell in love with the poems—the richness of humanity, the beauty, the absolute honesty. They're poems for anyone who's paying attention." And C. Bernard Jackson, the producer of the Los Angeles premiere, has commented, "Hard as I've tried to rid myself of all the pork accumulated as a 'boy child,' Carol Connolly comes along to remind me that were I to undergo an autopsy, they'd probably find an oink or two."

Also from Midwest Villages & Voices